Johnno
Greatest Moments

'Following Martin's triumphant return from the Rugby World Cup and subsequent retirement from international rugby, the Leicester Tigers Association committee, due to the swell of feeling from the supporters, unanimously proposed to put Martin forward for a testimonial year. No man has achieved more as a rugby player: captain of England, the Lions and Leicester Tigers. With each of these teams, under his leadership, he has achieved phenomenal success. A leader of men *par excellence*. Never a man more worthy of a testimonial year and I am delighted and honoured to be chairman of the Testimonial Committee.

'I would like to express my thanks to my committee who have given so much of their time and effort into organising what should be a very successful year for both Martin and the three charities: SPARKS, Macmillan Cancer Relief and NSPCC. The committee are: Stuart Henry, Neil McCorquodale, Gary Rooney, Robert Wilkinson and Eric Wood. I would also like to thank Jim Overend for doing such an excellent job managing the testimonial.'

Arthur Hazlerigg, Chairman of the Testimonial Committee

Copyright © 2004 Headline Book Publishing
Adapted from *Martin Johnson: The Autobiography* © 2003 Martin Johnson

First published in 2004
by HEADLINE BOOK PUBLISHING

10 9 8 7 6 5 4 3 2 1

Cataloguing in Publication Data is available from the British Library

ISBN 0 7553 1381 X

Typeset in Humanist
Printed and bound in Great Britain by Butler and Tanner

Headline's policy is to use papers that are natural, renewable and recyclable products and
made from wood grown in sustainable forests. The logging and manufacturing processes
are expected to conform to the environmental regulations of the country of origin.

Design by Butler and Tanner

Photographs courtesy of Actionimages and EMPICS

HEADLINE BOOK PUBLISHING
A division of Hodder Headline
338 Euston Road
London NW1 3BH

www.headline.co.uk
www.hodderheadline.com

foreword

I was delighted to accept a request to provide some words for Martin's testimonial book and I was politely asked to 'keep it brief'. I knew immediately that I'd struggle on that point. What can you say in a few words about someone who really has achieved so much in his career and has been there, done that and bought the T-shirt several times over?

Martin was a pleasure to work with in the six years he and I were together at international level. My view has always been that he is an outstanding ambassador for the game on and off the field and a great example of how a captain should lead his team.

There have been some superb England captains but I feel that Martin has been the best. He always led by example and he had the full respect of his team-mates and the coaching staff.

Martin was always open to new ideas and change when he was with England. Always prepared to speak his mind, he did so in an open and constructive manner and his feedback was invaluable to the plans and training sessions we put in place for the squad.

It was all of the above attributes which helped Martin become the great captain he was for England. Under him England lost just five times in thirty-nine games and he was a significant factor behind that success.

Everyone, quite rightly, will point to the highlights of 2003 as arguably the squad's and Martin's finest achievements as England captain. A Grand Slam, an unbeaten summer tour and the RWC win in Australia, but there were plenty of other games where Martin really did lead the team 'from the front'.

One game that immediately springs to mind was the 53-3 win over South Africa in 2002. Martin was superb that day and led the side brilliantly in difficult circumstances. The second Test against the same opposition in 2000 was also a game that brings back vivid memories as the two-Test series came after a defeat to Scotland just weeks previously.

After the win against South Africa in 2000, England went on a run of just three defeats out of 41 Tests and much of our success has to be credited to Johnno.

Martin's club career, of course, has been littered with success with five league championships and back-to-back Heineken Cup wins and I'm sure that the Leicester Tigers fans will support him throughout his richly deserved testimonial.

All the very best Johnno and a sincere 'thank you' from me and all the squad.

Sir Clive Woodward, OBE

TIGERS

BURNING BRIGHT

'I saw his first league match for the Tigers and
[he] sprinted on to the field, took up position
yards nearer to the opposition than he needed
to and glowered at them. Through England
caps and Lions tours, the expression has been
fixed. Perma-glower.'

1993 Cup winners

As the 1992-93 season got underway, Leicester started to develop a pack which would dominate English club rugby for almost a decade. I was twenty-two, my second-row partners Matt Poole and Neil Back were twenty-three. Dean Richards and John Wells were the only guys pushing thirty. Suddenly we had a young, exciting group of forwards, and with guys such as Rory and Tony Underwood, Stuart Potter and John Liley in our back line we began to look as though we might at last challenge Bath for the league title.

As it was, our season finished well, with a Cup final against a good Quinns side fair reward for our hard work. We beat them and I scored the winning try from a tap penalty move that had been handed down the generations at Leicester and which I have never seen work before or since. This was a major victory for us, our first silverware since the league title five years before.

'Leicester's powerful young lock, Martin Johnson, came charging up from a deep position and smashed clean through the middle to score by the posts.' John Reason, *Daily Telegraph*, April 1993

'Johnson crashed over for Tigers' crucial second-half try, and proved a continual menace to Quinns in the line-out with his height and power.' Chris Goddard, *Leicester Mercury*, April 1993

1995 champions

The 1994-95 season was a big one for Leicester, with the championship once again really down to us or Bath. We managed to get a draw at their place just after Christmas, which was the first time in some years we had come away from the Rec with any points at all. When we beat them in April at home

the title was almost in the bag. In World Cup year, though, there was an agreement that international players could appear in only a couple of matches in the last month of the league, so I sat out the clincher, our defeat of Bristol at Welford Road. Watching from the stands upset me a bit: I had started almost every game that season and to miss the one in which we were actually crowned champions was annoying. It was the first time the Tigers had won the league for seven years, finally breaking Bath's dominance which we had threatened to do for a couple of seasons. Things were looking good and we had plenty of youth in the team.

1999 champions

First up in the league we played Quinns, who had signed Zinzan Brooke. No one would have been piling into the bookies on our behalf, but we just clicked. We had real pace on the wing with Nnamdi Ezulike and Leon Lloyd, and we had Joel Stransky at No. 10 and Austin Healey at No. 9, behind probably the best pack in the league. We put forty-odd points on Quinns and carried on in that style, scoring heavily and hardly losing a game. We went down to Bedford, where Rory Underwood was now playing. We knew Rory liked to show people the outside when he was

'Not only has Martin been an inspiration to his fellow England players but also to every schoolboy who dreams one day of following in his footsteps and captaining his club and country.' RFU President Robert Horner

'It is safe to say that in my nine years at Leicester Tigers nobody in my eyes has stood out more as being wholeheartedly the worst drinker I have ever met. Not only did myself, Geordan Murphy and Leon Lloyd leave him at the bar one night dribbling into his pint glass, while twenty people stroked his rubber face, but to add insult to injury he was also beaten in a drinking race by my lovely girlfriend. Apart from that there are no other interesting stories about the "Forehead" that I can recall as he is such a dull old grumpy bastard!

'On a serious note – I hope he has a terrible testimonial season as he has got too much money already. MJ is the "Leicester Massive" through and through – an ultimate professional, a true legend and a gentleman of note/goofy freak.

'It's been a pleasure Johnno. Best of luck with your testimonial and all the very best for the future.' Leicester team-mate Lewis Moody

'If any aspirant seeks to play in the England second row, they could do no better than attend to the lessons laid down in Johnson's masterclass. Every aspect of tight-loose play was there: the rock-solid scrum, the authority at the line-out, but also the power generated ball in hand, the low driving position learnt as a youngster in New Zealand and the controlled aggression.' David Hands, *The Times*, November 1998 defending. We also knew Nnamdi had incredible pace. We told him what would happen and suggested he take it. Sure enough, early on we got the ball out wide, Rory showed Nnamdi the outside, Nnamdi took it and skinned him. He was lightning quick on the hard, early-season grounds.

Our team spirit was excellent and we were able to go up to Newcastle to win the league away from home. We had Matt Poole's stag do planned at Whitley Bay that weekend. Quite rightly, Dean had told us to cancel it, reminding us that we were playing for the title and he didn't want us distracted. 'Yes, you're right, Dean,' we said, but went on planning it in secret. The whole team stayed over in Newcastle that Sunday night. Some of the boys got up in the morning and went home, but the 'Whitley Bay 13' headed off to the coast for a legendary Bank Holiday Monday celebration of the club's third title – the first of the new era.

2001 The Double

The 2000-01 season was going to be a hell of a long haul. At Leicester, we were trying to win a historic third championship and we were also determined to do better in Europe. The season ticked along well and we were looking odds-on to retain the title and were going well in Europe, beating Pau 20-3 away – never easy – and getting through the group stages to set up a quarter-final clash with Swansea, which we went on to win fairly comfortably. We were dumped out of the Tetley's Bitter Cup by Harlequins, which was disappointing, but at least that gave us breathing space to concentrate on the two bigger competitions.

With two matches still to go, we blew away a weakened Newcastle Falcons 51-7. All we needed was for Bath to beat Wasps, our nearest championship challengers, in a match later the same day. We sat in a room at the clubhouse, praying for a Bath victory – strange

'One man stood alone, head bowed, hands on knees, reflecting in solitude on the magnitude of the achievement. He had led England to epic victory; he had led the British Lions to history in South Africa but yesterday in France he led his club to the promised land – the pinnacle of European rugby. His name is Martin Johnson. When the England and Lions captain reflects on his mighty career, he will remember the day the Parc des Princes became the Park of the Tigers.' Rupert Bates, *Daily Telegraph*, May 2001

'Leicester gave English rugby one of its greatest moments, including internationals, by lifting the Heineken Cup and becoming champions of Europe with a performance of such courage and deadly late devil that it was all scarcely credible. It goes without saying that this was the greatest day in Leicester's history; it sealed their team's true worth and sealed the future of professional club rugby. Nothing less.'

Stephen Jones, *Sunday Times*, May 2001

feeling – and cursing them when Wasps took what seemed like a winning lead. But Mike Catt scored late on to give them the win, our fans, hanging on after the Falcons game in the hope of celebrating the title, going mad in the main bar below. We then went on to win the Zurich Championship by beating Bath in the final at Twickenham.

However, our season was not quite over. Having completed a domestic double, the biggest club prize of all was within our grasp – we had a European Cup final against Stade Français, at the old Parc des Princes in Paris. I was struggling and in pain with a stiff neck, injured in our semi-final against Gloucester, but everyone had knocks and niggles. All our walking wounded would make it on to the pitch. We knew Stade would be very tough to beat, especially in their home city. They were packed with quality players and French sides are always stronger at home, so it was going to be a massive game.

It was a nervy changing room when the referee called us out and a heavy atmosphere once we got on to the pitch. The Stade players walked over and started squaring up to us. Our players went to meet them and the atmosphere got very charged, to the point where I thought it might all kick off before the game even started.

The game itself was clean though. It was a cagey first half, both sides kicking for territory. They were ahead at half time, but we defended very well, keeping their big runners at bay. We certainly felt we were well in contention and that if we got a score early on we could take control. Mind you, I didn't expect it to come just forty-eight seconds after the restart, when Pat Howard chipped through, Geordan Murphy kicked it on and Leon Lloyd beat the defenders to score. Bang! We were right back in the game. It was a big confidence boost. I was binned for slapping one of their players, but the guys conceded just three points in the ten minutes, which was a brilliant effort. Backy scored from close range once I got back on, but their fly-half Dominguez was keeping them in it and they nudged ahead as the game neared the end.

'That the Parc refreshes parts that other stadiums fail to reach was evident even before boot had been put to ball when Leicester formed a phalanx around Martin Johnson and advanced menacingly on the Stade players as they ran on to the pitch. The Leicester body language was unmistakeable: this may be your turf, but it's going to be ours today.' Nick Cain, *Sunday Times*, May 2001

Then a great break and a superb pass by Austin Healey put Leon Lloyd in again to give us a 32-30 lead. We needed the conversion though – we couldn't risk them winning a penalty or finding space for a drop goal in the remaining minutes. Stimpson kicked brilliantly from the touchline and the sight of the ball sailing between the posts will go down as one of the all-time great moments in Leicester history. They made a last-gasp break at the death, but we snuffed it out. We were European Champions.

It had been a frenetic, explosive, end-to-end match and a great advertisement for European rugby. I was exhausted and exhilarated all at once. The whole squad, even the guys who were not on the bench, ran straight on to the pitch to celebrate. We saluted our fantastic supporters, hoisting the cup on a lap round the pitch, before heading for the changing room to soak everything up. To win the European Cup in Paris was the biggest and best day of my club career. Could we do it again?

2002 The double Double

We were chasing a fourth consecutive Premiership title. We were also looking to become the first club to retain the European Cup.

However, our season didn't start well and we lost on the opening day to Newcastle. Our coach, Dean Richards, had been talking about giving the Lions players a rest, but with Wasps up next he sat myself, Martin Corry, Neil Back and Austin Healey on the bench. It was close for sixty minutes or so, but just as we started to get on top, he brought on the experienced players and we ended up running away with it. The same thing happened at Gloucester the following week and I enjoyed those twenty-minute run-outs in the autumn sun. We carried on pretty much unhindered and by

'He's top shelf. He's obviously good at set pieces, but he adds to that. He's pretty quick around the paddock and, at one stage, I think he had the top tackle count for England. That's unusual for a tight forward.' Duncan Hall, former Australian lock and Leicester forwards coach

Christmas people were starting to say a fourth league title was a foregone conclusion. We never took that view, although that was how it turned out.

In the European Cup, Llanelli jolted us in the group stages, getting to within three points of us in a 12–9 clash. They surprised us with how good a team they were. A mate who had seen the game said afterwards it was strange watching us having to dig deep at home, because we usually had it in the bag with fifteen minutes to go. That was a real wake-up call. We beat Calvisano away, but I missed our trip to Perpignan with my broken hand. Perpignan's visit to Welford Road started with the visitors scoring a try in the first minute and ended with us putting fifty points on them in one of the best displays of club rugby I have seen. With just Calvisano at home and Llanelli away to come, we had virtually qualified for the quarter-finals. The Italians came and went without troubling us too much, but we came

'The England lock was, yet again, simply outstanding at Franklin's Gardens on Saturday. The Allied Dunbar Premiership is now within Leicester's grasp after they opened up an eight-point lead on their nearest challengers, Northampton, and Johnson's implacable attitude, his utter refusal to compromise any aspect of his game, will ensure they do not stumble during the six-match run-in to the title. "He is probably the best forward England have got, if not the best in Europe," Dean Richards, the Leicester team manager, said. This is typical understatement; Johnson is up there with John Eales, of Australia, as one of the world's best tight forwards.'
David Hands, *The Times*, March 1999

'When it comes to selecting teams, either as a supporter, coach or even as a player, it is always nice to have one or two players that you can pen in from the start and know that this player is the best in the world in all ways. Johnno has always been that player. If you are going to war in the biggest game ever or playing a friendly testimonial match, Johnno is the man that you want leading you into battle. When the opposition read the team sheet and see his name, they know it is going to be hard, tough and uncompromising – the way it should be on the rugby field.

'Johnno was the rock around which many a successful team was built, and not just because of his ability as a player. His burning desire to succeed and the attitude he displayed sucked other players along with him and, coupled with his decision-making ability, made him one of the greatest captains of all time. For Martin to hold the William Webb Ellis Trophy aloft as captain of the Rugby World Cup champions was a deserved and fitting moment for the man who has contributed so much to club and country, and the wonderful game of rugby union.

'Congratulations on a spectacular career Johnno, and all the best in your future endeavours.' Joel Stransky, former Leicester team-mate and RWC winner with the Springboks heavily unstuck at Stradey Park. They needed to win to qualify and came at us very hard, outplaying us like we hadn't been outplayed in a long, long time. It was try-less, but they deserved their 24–12 win and it was a fairly humbling experience.

We had won five and lost just one, normally enough to guarantee a home quarter-final, but lots of teams had been very successful, winning six out of six, and we were relieved to find we had squeaked it. We beat Leinster at home in the quarters and then found we had come up against Llanelli again in the semis. I was worried and anxious about that match. They had played well in the line-outs and scrum in both games, and, with powerful runners like Scotty Quinnell, Martin Madden and Chris Wyatt, they had broken our defence, which we pride ourselves on. Also, Stephen Jones, their fly-half, was a metronomic penalty kicker who could punish you from pretty much anywhere inside

your half. However, we had one advantage because it was to be a 'home' tie, with the match played in England, and not too far away at Nottingham Forest's City Ground. We knew we would have plenty of support, although the Scarlets brought thousands of their fans, too, creating a full house and a fantastic atmosphere.

At their ground in the group stages they had attacked us continually, running the ball at us from everywhere – close in, out wide, with pace and power. That Sunday afternoon they were a lot quieter. We managed to bottle Quinnell and Madden up – Madden and I clashed heads as he charged at me full on, both of us ending up face down on the turf. I got up rapidly, determined to beat him to my feet, although I was still a little woozy and staggered a couple of paces before coming to my senses. We played some decent, committed rugby and once the initial moments were over I always felt we were going to win.

We had spotted that their defence was staying very wide and thought we might profit from a pick-and-go. Sure enough, Harry Ellis, our young scrum-half, scampered over from about twenty yards, straight through the middle of a ruck, but we could never quite get clear of them. For all the pressure we placed on them, I don't think we were ever awarded a penalty in their half and that was very unusual. Close to the end, we did eventually win a penalty – just inside our own half and quite a way out on the right-hand side. I was heading over to Rod Kafer to discuss what line-out move we should go for when we kicked it into touch, when I saw Stimmo pointing at the posts. Nothing I could do – the ref had already signalled. It was a very difficult kick and it was a brave call by Stimmo. It was one of those – pot it and you're a hero, miss it, and you're the villain. He managed to get it over, pinballing it between the posts and the bar, to give us the game, 13-12.

In the history of European Cups only

'Leicester became the first team to retain the Heineken Cup in a wondrous occasion at the Millennium stadium yesterday, in a match that never flowed and never wove pretty patterns, but was filled with such gallantry and ferocity that you winced, even up in the stands. Martin Johnson lifted the trophy on a podium in the middle of the field to mark a day for Leicester that, in its historic way, was the equal of their triumph in a superior match in the final in Paris last year.' Stephen Jones, *Sunday Times,* May 2002

Brive have made two finals on the trot. It is a tough call to do it once. Defending the title, with everyone desperate to beat you, while you are trying to compete domestically as well, is incredibly hard. The Millennium Stadium is one of the world's great sporting venues and Munster, our opponents, have some of rugby's most noisy, colourful fans. Bursting at the seams with thousands of Leicester's green-clad fans and even more red jerseys from the Irish province, it was an awesome place, with a tremendous atmosphere, on the day of the final.

Munster were going to be a tough side to beat but we thought we would be able to pressurise their line-out, and ultimately our edge in that area, and the pressure we were able to exert on them could have been what made the difference in the game. It was a tense affair, which Munster led 6–5 at the break, Geordan Murphy providing our points. But when Austin Healey broke away in the second half for the crucial try, which Stimmo converted, it gave us an eventual 15–9 win. If the Stade win had been pure jubilation, the Munster victory was as much about relief as joy. You could almost feel the weight lift off your shoulders. We had wanted so desperately to keep the title and had battled so hard, particularly against Llanelli, that a loss would have been disastrous. As it was, we had become probably the most successful club side in the world.

'There are two types of captain. The one who says do what I do, who is always on the ball and never shirks, and the yapper, the one who's always talking but is not always up front. Martin is a "follow me, let's do it" type. He'll play hard and expect others to do the same.'

Duncan Hall, former Australian lock and Leicester forwards coach

LIONS ROAR

'Johnno, you're a legend and a fantastic rugby player. I remember when you arrived in NZ as a replacement for Wade Dooley during the 1993 Lions tour I thought that we had someone special with us and so it proved as you forced your way into the second and third Tests and played extremely well. Captain of the next two Lions tours and World Cup-winning captain tells its own story and seeing a smile on your face in Australia said to me that even you enjoyed it. Many congratulations to a true great.' Gavin Hastings, former Scotland captain and ex-Lions team-mate

There are few greater honours in rugby than to be selected to play for the British and Irish Lions. Players from four countries, enemies under other circumstances, coming together to take on the world's best on the other side of the planet, is a unique tradition in sport. The fact that they only ever play in rugby's traditional southern hemisphere strongholds has always added to that incredible aura.

1993

By 1993, and the tour to New Zealand, I was on the fringes of the England squad. However, I felt that, realistically, I had no serious chance of making the trip. The club structure throughout the British Isles at that time was not particularly competitive or well organised. How could you select someone for a Lions tour on the basis of a game between Melrose and Hawick? With no other way of judging ability or potential, the Lions' selectors almost always chose guys who had played plenty of Test rugby in the Five Nations.

I had played just one international so, while the Lions headed south, I went to Canada with a young England squad. The Canadians were a strong, aggressive and talented bunch who had given the All Blacks a tough game in the quarter-final of the 1991 Rugby World Cup. We lost the first Test but won the second, which was a really good result in the circumstances.

After that second match we were having a 'court' session – a long-standing rugby tour tradition involving 'fining' players with alcohol for amusing and spurious offences – when we got

'To me, there is no doubt that he has been the outstanding world figure in rugby over the past few years.'
Ian McGeechan, former Northampton, Scotland and Lions coach

'If there is one rugby player who has total and unequivocal respect in every country around the world it is Martin Johnson. It is safe to say I rate Martin, as a player, captain and person, at the top of the tree.

'For me, as a coach, it was a privilege to work with him. I take some satisfaction from being the person to first select him as captain back in 1997 – and what a year that turned out to be! But I have to admit it wasn't rocket science on my part. At that time I was coaching Northampton and it was obvious the effect Martin had on his team-mates, the opposition and the game, and it was that personality I wanted to "front-up" the Lions in South Africa, and yes, when it came to tossing the coin, Springbok captain Gary Teichmann had to look up to Martin Johnson. Johnno's desire to succeed has rubbed off on and made better players of those who have played with him.

'For me, he has been the outstanding player of his generation and rates as one of the most influential players in the game of all time. He has been to Leicester Tigers, England and the Lions what Colin Meads was to New Zealand rugby.

'Martin has lifted a number of trophies in his career, but I was genuinely delighted to see him finish his international career with a smile on his face and the Webb Ellis Trophy above his head.

'Thanks Johnno, for an unbelievable contribution to rugby and for making me and millions of others experience the joy of success through your efforts – a man of few words but hugely significant actions. We all owe you.

'Congratulations and I wish you and your family much enjoyment and success in the future.'
Ian McGeechan

the news that Wade Dooley's father had died. Wade was flying home from the Lions tour and I was being called down to New Zealand. Tremendously excited, I was thoroughly stitched up in the session, with the 'judge', Chris Oti, fining me heavily for leaving the England tour early. After a few fines I started giving the judge some grief, with the result that I was fined again, and it all turned into a horrible vicious circle. Fairly smashed, I caught my flight home, but I don't recall much of it.

After a quick turnaround back in England, Vince Cunningham – who was replacing Scott Hastings who had smashed his cheekbone – and I arrived in Christchurch before the main tour party who had been playing the midweek game ahead of the first Test. Next day we were straight into it, hitting tackle bags in a training session with Dick Best. This was way ahead of anything I had been involved in before. Canada had been a tough tour on the pitch, but it had taken place in a non-rugby country,

so there had been no off-field pressure. Here I was in New Zealand training with the likes of Brian Moore and Peter Winterbottom – a guy whom, as an eleven-year-old, I had watched make his England debut. I kept my head down, tried to work hard and endeavoured to win the respect of my team mates.

I sat in the stands and watched the first Test, which the guys lost through a Grant Fox kick towards the end. The start of the tour had gone fairly well – they had come back from way behind to beat the Maoris, for instance – but the wheels were starting to come off at this point.

The day after the first Test we travelled up to play Taranaki. I had faced them for King Country a year or two earlier – we had beaten them in one of our bigger performances – and now I made my Lions debut on their ground. There was a big, partisan crowd and the Taranaki lads were very pumped up. We were poor in the first half, but

Ben Clarke came off the bench and played brilliantly to help us win 49–25 in the end.

I had played reasonably well, but I was surprised to be selected for the weekend's big game, a clash with Auckland at Eden Park on the Saturday.

We started well, but Auckland wore us down and as the game progressed we suffered a few injuries and made a few mistakes to lose out 23–18. It was my first really big game for the Lions and I felt I played OK against Robin Brooke, whom I regarded as the world's best front-jumping second row.

Then it was the second Test. It was do or die. If we lost that game, the series was lost and the tour would have turned into an absolute disaster. I was

named with Martin Bayfield in the second row. That was a fantastic feeling. Ten years earlier I had dreamed of playing in a Test match for the Lions, but had never thought it would happen. I remember getting to the stadium and feeling very nervous. I had one Test match under my belt and felt like I was heading into the unknown.

It was a fast and furious game, with the key moment coming when Fitzpatrick lost the ball in contact. It was quickly transferred to Rory Underwood on the wing and he out-sprinted the cover to score in the corner. They tried to come back, but we held them off to record a memorable victory by 20–7. That was a brilliant moment. Any win against the All Blacks on their own patch is a big win, but the Lions had

'Martin Johnson is the all-time great England player. You come across his class only once in a generation.' Former Lions coach Fran Cotton

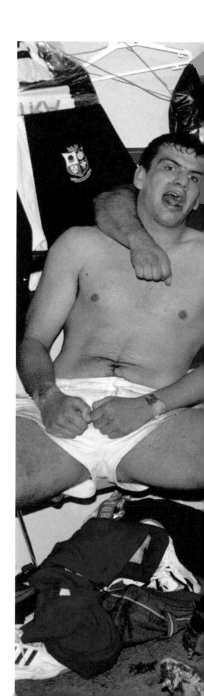

not won there since 1977 and, in context of the tour, this was a huge result. We had a chance to win the series.

The All Blacks changed their team a little for the third Test and their crowd, stung by the defeat and by the masses of Lions fans appearing in their own back yard, was suddenly right behind them. The match was played with huge intensity. After fifteen or so minutes we were 10–0 up, but they got back into it with tries before half-time. I am a little hazy on the details. A fight erupted at a breakdown and Martin Bayfield took a huge, haymaking swing at one of their guys, missed and smacked me instead. Had it been an opposition punch I would either have ducked it or seen it coming and been able to deflect some of the force. As it was, it came, not surprisingly, out of the blue. It was the latest in a number of concussions I had received and, although I played on, much of the rest of the game is a blur. I remember having to ask what our line-out calls meant, a sure sign I was in trouble, and hazily coming round towards the end of the match with the All Blacks about to win the game 30–13 and, with it, the series.

It was a disappointed dressing room afterwards. We had had our chances but it had not happened. From a personal point of view, I would have to say the tour was a success. I had played reasonably well in the two Tests considering I was lucky to be there at all. In fact I was lucky to get my first England cap earlier that year, without which I would not have been made a reserve.

Four years later, things were a little different.

1997

As the 1996-97 season wore on the talk turned towards the forthcoming Lions tour. Much of it was very negative. The South Africans were world champions.

'Johnson was everything you could wish a Lions captain to be.' Stephen Jones, *Sunday Times*, June 1997

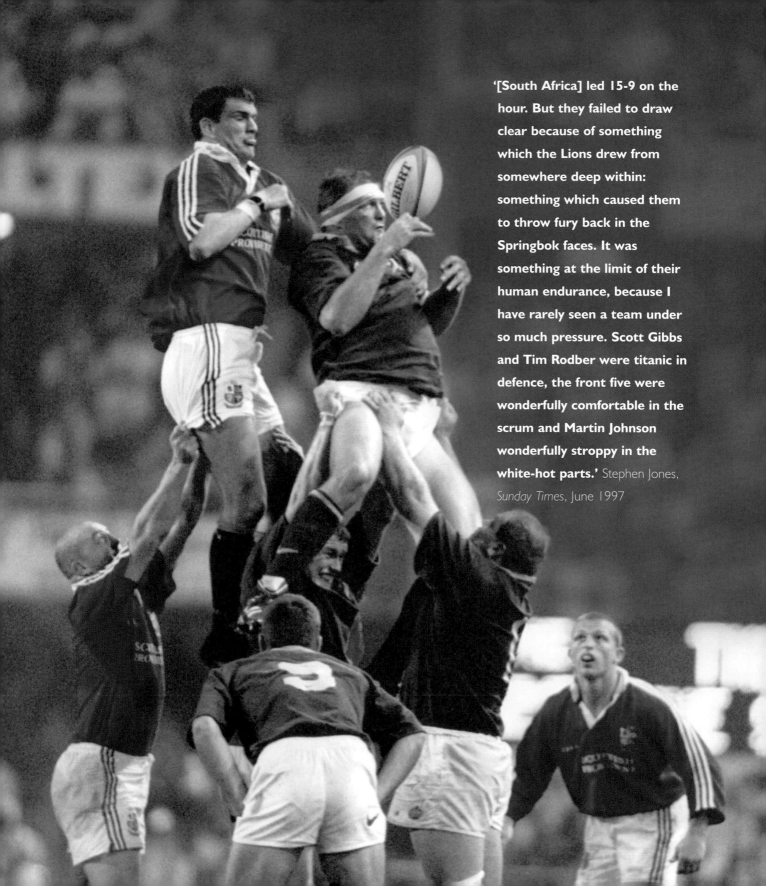

'[South Africa] led 15-9 on the hour. But they failed to draw clear because of something which the Lions drew from somewhere deep within: something which caused them to throw fury back in the Springbok faces. It was something at the limit of their human endurance, because I have rarely seen a team under so much pressure. Scott Gibbs and Tim Rodber were titanic in defence, the front five were wonderfully comfortable in the scrum and Martin Johnson wonderfully stroppy in the white-hot parts.' Stephen Jones, *Sunday Times*, June 1997

'To me, Martin Johnson during his international career has been three very different things.

'I met Johnno at the age of eighteen when I joined the England squad for the first time. I found him deeply intimidating. And every time I have played against him since, he has become more so! At a massive six foot-plus, and with the ferrangi brow, is bad enough, but knowing just what an effect he always has on his team-mates has made matters even worse.

'This brings me on to Martin Johnson the inspiration. Few words have had such an enormous impact on me than those he has delivered in his unique (swearing/aggressive) way in England's changing-rooms and on the fields of play. It is impossible to impress upon you the level of confidence I have built up purely by knowing that he is in our changing-room and that he is leading our team.

'Johnno is a fantastic person and a great friend. In the England team hotel he is forever checking to see that I am alright even when the weight of the country's expectation must have been crushing his shoulders. Making sure everyone else was happy, when the pressure on him was at its worst, illustrates what an unselfish and thoughtful gentleman he is.

'A great sense of humour and a great leader and team man; I have learnt more from my time playing alongside MJ than I ever had time to repay. Probably most importantly, what it really takes to be successful, how to fight three people at once and how to get the ref on your side at the same time as calling him a bell-end – you can't ask for more.

'It is no coincidence that Johnno has done pretty much everything in the game and won it too. Lions tours, European Cups, League Cups, Grand Slams and the World Cup. It has been an absolute privilege to have played in his team in what is his era and to have the personal honour of saying "I know him well".

'Best of luck with the testimonial season mate, nobody deserves it more than you.'
Jonny Wilkinson, England and Lions team-mate and fellow RWC winner

They were a powerful, skilful and established team who were playing well. Most people seemed to assume the tour would end in a thrashing for the Lions and humiliation for northern hemisphere rugby.

The other area of speculation surrounded the captaincy of the party. There was not really an obvious candidate. To my surprise, in March my name started being bandied around. Obviously the skipper had to be someone who would make the Test team and I seemed to have a good chance of that, but I had relatively little leadership experience and none at international level.

I was in a hotel in Gloucester when I got a phone call from the BBC journalist Ian Robertson. 'You probably already know this, Martin, but congratulations on being made captain of the Lions.'

Eyebrows were raised in some sections of the media and elsewhere at my appointment. I was viewed – am still viewed in some quarters – as a bit of a Midlands Neanderthal: grumpy, unfriendly and monosyllabic. How would I handle the most important part of the job – the after-dinner speaking? I knew at the time that this was ridiculous but, looking back, it seems utterly bizarre. I might not be

'I don't think they could have picked a better man for a Lions captain. He's a gentleman and very humble, but he'll surprise a few because he can be very strong if you don't do what's expected of you.'

Noel McQuilkin, coach of King Country

the most polished performer out there, and I probably won't go on to host game shows when I retire, but I thought I could manage 'Ladies and gentlemen, Mr President, thank you very much.' Anyway, who gave a stuff?

The Springbok press and public didn't give us a chance of winning the series and our own press and public were not much more confident; after all, we had all been weaned on a diet of southern hemisphere supremacy. However, we had an excellent management and coaching set-up and a very good side. No tour party containing the likes of Jason Leonard, Jerry Guscott, Lawrence Dallaglio, Rob Howley, Neil Jenkins, Ieuan Evans, Rob Wainwright, Gregor Townsend and Keith Wood is going to be a pushover and the league returnees added a great deal. With union having just turned professional, the rest of us were really just amateurs with money. They knew a lot more about what it

was really like to train hard and play for your living.

The weekend before the first international we beat Natal 42–12. It was after that win that the home press and public started to sit up and take notice of us.

I got the feeling that the Springboks thought they were going to win that first Test. Maybe that was not surprising. They were on their way to becoming one of the great all-time teams with seventeen consecutive wins around the corner, and they were at home. However, their complacency cost them dearly as we managed to beat them 25–16. Matt Dawson scored one of our tries with an outrageous dummy, and Alan Tait the other, with Neil Jenkins' five penalties keeping the Boks at bay.

I remember a great little moment in the changing rooms afterwards. Obviously everyone was delighted with the win. We had played well in every area, including the scrum, where, after being knocked back badly at the first engagement, we had gained parity and even started to impose ourselves towards the end. I am sitting there, trying to think sensibly: we mustn't let the success go to our heads, we need to stay calm and focus on the next Test, let's not celebrate until we win the next Test, and so on. Scotty Gibbs seemed to be thinking along the same lines. 'No way are we going to lie down against those boys next week Johnno,' he was saying. 'No way.' I looked up and there was Scotty standing in his pants, with a fag in one hand and a can of beer in the other. I had to grin. 'At least you're saying the right things, Gibbsy!' I thought. He meant it, though.

We knew the Springboks would come back strongly in the second Test, and we were right. They had three game plans and all of them were to come at us hard. It was rocky out there for the first few minutes. Early on there was a break for a penalty and Lawrence Dallaglio and I looked across at each other, both raising our eyebrows. We certainly knew we were in a match as the Boks threw everything they had at us.

'Johnson was chosen as captain by Ian McGeechan simply because he was Johnson. He was picked not so much to lead but to be himself, to inspire by relentless example. Even in an intimidating Test series against an intimidating team, it was still Johnson in red who appeared to have the psychological edge over anybody in Springbok green.' Stephen Jones, *Sunday Times*, June 2001

The defining moment came at 15–15. A ruck formed after a tackle and we pretty much gave it up for dead. If you watch the video, you'll see that we are all hanging back – all apart from Neil Back, who got in there and nicked the ball in the way he does. The ball found its way to Keith Wood, who shoed it up the touchline. It was recycled back to Jerry Guscott, unmarked in midfield. He looked up, swung his right boot and dropped it over to make it 18–15 to us. The next five minutes were among the most tense of my life as we defended against wave after wave of South African attacks.

That final whistle was a marvellous moment. Guys were hugging each other, screaming and laughing. The feeling of elation was remarkable. They had scored three tries to nil. Fifteen of our points came from Jenks' boot. Some said it was a moral victory for them, but that's rubbish. Every penalty they gave away stopped us from attacking – and who knows whether we would have crossed from any of those positions? Tries are nice, but all that matters is the numbers on the board. And they say we won.

And so to the third and final Test. Mentally, it was very hard for us to pick ourselves up for that game. I went out to warm up and all the nerves and anxiety I had experienced before the previous two matches had vanished. We played some good rugby and, having slipped behind, battled our way back to the point where, if we had been hungry and desperate for the result, we might have got into contention to win. But, as the cliché

'Captain Johnson, who enjoyed his best game on tour when it was most needed, called all the non-playing reserves on to the field to share the moment.' Brendan Gallagher, *Daily Telegraph*, June 1997

has it, they wanted it more than we did, winning 35–16.

It had been a hell of a tough tour, with a number of players suffering injuries, but also a phenomenally successful one. All the talk about the Lions being finished as a concept in the professional era vanished almost overnight. Instead, they were rightly acclaimed as being one of the world's greatest sporting traditions.

Ahead, four years away, was Australia and many people's thoughts turned there almost immediately.

2001

I never took for granted that I would be going on my third tour, particularly since I had spent much of 2000 perhaps not exactly in the international wilderness, but somewhere that felt not too far from it. As it was, I was named as captain.

With the serious action not far away, the Aussie media were starting to get stuck into us. A headline in *The Australian* read, 'McBain labels Lions boring' and quoted the Queensland coach, Mark McBain, attacking our style of play. In particular, he seemed to think we played too forward-oriented a game. 'The rolling maul … it's just not a spectacle, is it?' he had apparently said.

I found that a bit odd, given that we had scored thirty-one tries in two outings at that point, twenty of them by our backs and a number of the forwards' scores coming not from mauls but from loose play. I hoped, too, that we would be able to make him eat his words in the upcoming match against Brisbane and we did just that, running out 42–8 winners.

Tour result up to that point? Three games, three wins. Things looked good.

The night before the first Test,

however, the team meeting was alive with nerves and pressure. I have never known so anxious a bunch of guys. I think it was due to a combination of factors. Australia were world champions and formidable opponents. Thousands of people had spent a lot of money travelling halfway around the world to watch us. The media presence and interest was huge. The whole thing felt enormous.

But the game could hardly have started better. We won a line-out on the halfway line in the third minute. Danny Grewcock caught it and gave quick ball off the top to Rob Howley. Rob passed to Jonny, who missed out Hendo to find O'Driscoll. He was brought down by Nathan Grey 35m out, but managed to throw the ball back out of the tackle. Howley scooped the ball up brilliantly off his feet, and formed the ruck as he was tackled by George Smith. Scott Quinnell picked up and popped it short to Wilko, who handed it on to Matt Perry. Pezza, with soft

'Not until you play with him do you really appreciate how hard the man is. A born leader – playing alongside him was the ultimate experience.' Former Lions team-mate Brian O'Driscoll

and very quick hands in the face of an on-rushing defender, passed the ball to Jason Robinson, steaming up outside him. Jase was still a few yards outside their twenty-two and the full-back, Chris Latham, thinking he had him covered, showed him the outside. Big mistake: Robinson's awesome step and explosive pace took him straight past a diving Latham to the line.

The whole move had taken just eighteen seconds and with two minutes and forty-four seconds on the clock we were five points up. The Lions supporters in the crowd were

going wild as Robinson ran round behind the posts, punching the air and screaming, before disappearing under a pile of red shirts. It was a dream start, just what we had wanted, and gave us the belief that we could penetrate what was then the world's best defence. Our second try came off a scrum in the thirty-fourth minute. We went right and Rob Howley fed Brian O'Driscoll, who stepped through the Wallabies' blind side defence. Robinson had come across to make the extra man and he passed on to Daf James who scored in the corner. It was especially pleasing because this was a set move.

Half time and the score was still close: 12-3. In the changing room, the nerves had gone and we felt good, but the Wallabies do not panic and we knew we had to keep the heat on – something we did straight after the restart. From a maul within the first minute, the ball was smuggled back to O'Driscoll, still inside our own half. He set off on an amazing run; stepping, feinting and shrugging off tackles, he sprinted on to touch down between the posts. It was one of the best tries scored in a Lions shirt. In any shirt.

Still, we couldn't relax. In the fiftieth minute, we kicked for touch after winning a penalty. Martin Corry took the line-out ball and Rob Henderson beat tackles from Larkham, Burke and Roff before finally being dropped 5m out by John Eales. The ruck formed, Howley gave it short to Balshaw, but he was held up. A second ruck, and Scotty Quinnell picked up and drove, taking Burke and Toutai Kefu over with him. Four tries to nil, Jonny converts to make it 29–3. Scarcely more than half the game gone, and we are in dreamland.

They came back to score two consolation tries, but we held on to win 29–13. Sitting there in the changing room, basking in the warmth of a win, everyone together, relaxing and joking, is the best time you get as a player. I said to the guys, 'This is what it's all about, winning these games … everyone's a part of this.'

Just before the second Test, in Melbourne, Donal Lenihan laid out the opportunity for us, 'The Lions are 125

years old and in all that time, only once have they achieved back-to-back Test series wins, in 1971 and 1974.' It was in our hands to be the second Lions side to do so.

We started the match pretty much as we had left off, breaking apart the much-vaunted Wallaby defence almost at will. We could have scored very early had Daf James spotted Jason Robinson outside him as he was tackled close to their line. As it was he didn't, knocking on as he was brought down. That set the tone for our performance. We went ahead through a Neil Back try from a catch-and-drive, but as the halfway stage approached we led narrowly, 11–3. I felt that if we played the same way in the second half the match, and the series, were ours.

And we were great – for the first thirty seconds. We won the kick-off and drove the ball back at them, making a lot of yards. Then Jonny Wilkinson took the ball up the blind side and tried

to throw a pass over the top of their defender. Joe Roff intercepted to score in the corner and the downhill slide began. It was a turning point in the match because it lifted them and knocked us back, but it was not *the* turning point. If we had replied quickly it would not have mattered.

We tried hard to fight our way back into contention, but kept making silly individual errors, turning the ball over and giving away penalties – all of which added to the Wallabies' momentum. The game ended 35–14, a record defeat for the Lions against Australia.

The third Test, played in Sydney's magnificent Stadium Australia, was another fast-paced affair. We swapped penalties early on and were soon 9–3 behind, but I felt good and thought that we were well in the game.

The second half started very well, with Jonny diving over, the conversion making it 20–16. We should have gone on from

there to kill the game off. Instead, we suffered from a moment of madness from Colin Charvis. In our half and with no support, Colin took a quick line-out to himself and suddenly realised he had nowhere to go. With Australian attackers bearing down on him he tried to hoof it clear, but his kick was horrible and the Wallabies built a position from which Herbert scored his second. Burke converted to make the score 23–20. Herbert was sin-binned for a high tackle on O'Driscoll, but we failed to add to our score while he was off. A Jonny Wilkinson penalty made it level with twenty minutes to go, but two more penalties gave the Aussies a 29–23 lead.

We needed a converted try to win. We kept pressing and pressing, creating two golden opportunities right at the death. Two minutes to go and we won an attacking line-out around 5m out. If we took our own ball we had a chance to drive them over or win a penalty try if they pulled down the maul, as they had been doing throughout the series. I called the throw to me and got up OK, but Justin Harrison came up in front of me and got both hands on the ball to nick it.

The ball was cleared, but we brought it right back at them. The hooter went and it came down to whether we could get over their line before the ball went dead. We were in their twenty-two and they couldn't afford to infringe, because the referee can't end the game on a defensive penalty. The ball was recycled and recycled and suddenly it moved out towards their left corner, reaching Matt Perry. A charging Iain Balshaw was coming up on his right shoulder at full pace. If the ball went to his hands he was in … but Pezza's pass went slightly behind Balsh, he lost momentum and the ball was turned over. Walker ran it into touch and the game was over.

In some matches – thankfully not many – you are well beaten and you know it. This time we could have won the match, and with it the series, right up until the last moment. Despite the negatives, I am proud to have been on the tour and proud to have led the boys. We played some great rugby in the first test and in the first half of the second. Immediately after the final game I said we couldn't have asked for any more from the players who finished that match.

'Johnson is one of the few certainties in the ever-changing modern game. There is an honesty and sincerity within him that does not waiver, no matter what the circumstances or the pressure. He has commitment infused into every pore. There is a code of honour in all that he does. He does not shirk responsibility, nor should those around him. There are the tenets he has abided by since he first played the game over twenty years ago.' Mick Cleary, *Daily Telegraph*, April 2004

SWEET CHARIOT

'How often the word legend is thrown about
when describing people and it is only when
someone like **Martin Johnson** carries that
title that you are forced to reconsider others
who have been called a legend. It was always
a true "test" when playing against **Martin**
and that is the biggest compliment I can pay
him. **Johnno,** when you walk away from
rugby, know that you made a difference.
Congratulations on a marvellous career.
Cheers.' Mark Andrews, most-capped South
African Test forward

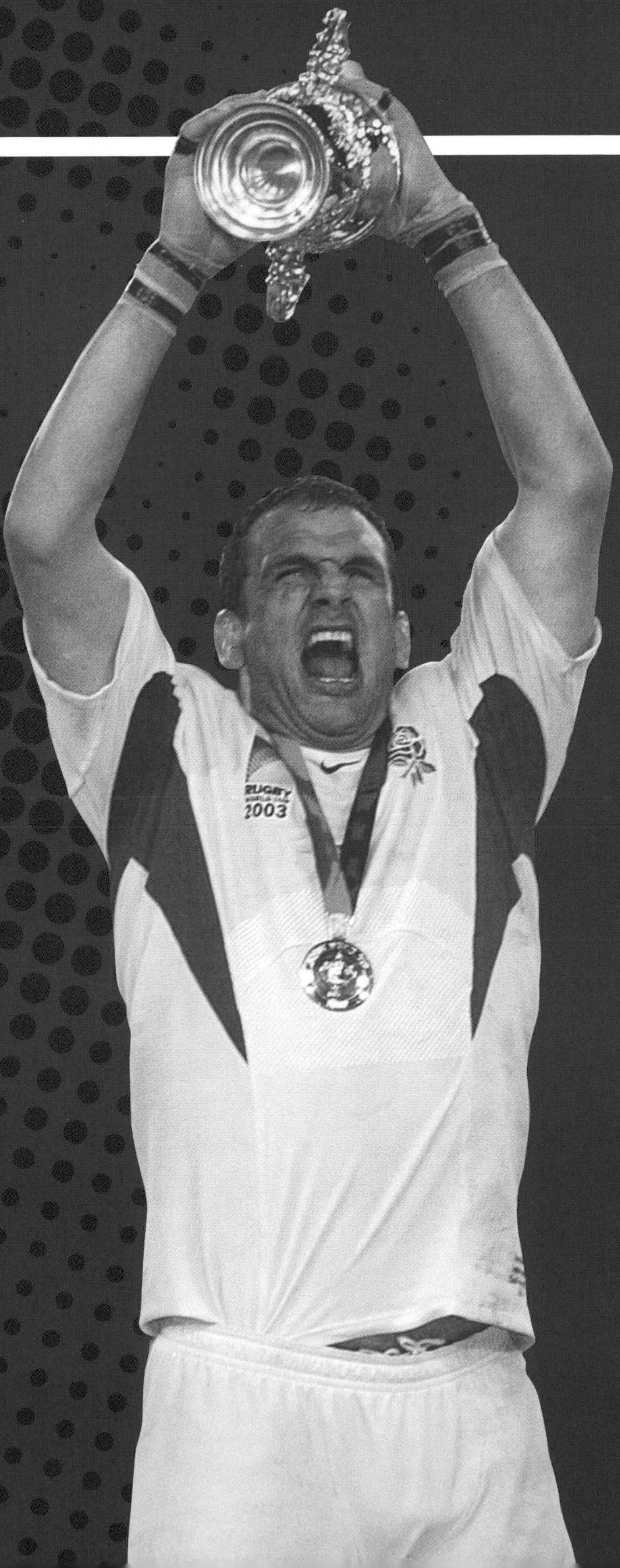
RUGBY
2003

Debut

In the autumn of 1992, South Africa toured and I had no expectations of being selected. Wade Dooley and Martin Bayfield played in the second row. Nothing changed for the Six Nations. France were first up, trying to stop a third consecutive English Grand

'When he stepped into the England team for the first time, it was obvious immediately that the 23-year-old had presence. People spoke in hushed tones about the honing of his skills he received when he played as a youngster in New Zealand. Here was an All Black among our own ranks. He turned out to be a man beyond even the intransigence of that fabled breed.'
Michael Aylwin, *Guardian*, November 2003

Slam. The day before that game, I was up in Leicester with the B team, preparing to play France B. We had trained in the morning and were just about to have a pre-lunch meeting when Peter Rossborough, the B-team manager, pulled me to one side. He said he had just had word from London that Wade was a slight injury doubt with a thigh strain. They wanted me to head down there to cover for him. I thought that was a bit strange. It was less than twenty-four hours to kick-off. By then, normally, you're either fit or you're not.

I think Peter must have known I was going to play, but I guess he wanted me to get down there and hear it officially. It certainly hadn't dawned on me at that stage. At that age, I was quite young in some ways, perhaps a bit naïve and not particularly self-confident, so it was daunting enough just to be asked to travel down.

In a bit of a daze, I nipped home to get my car to drive down. I slowly started to twig that maybe I would be playing. There was an outside chance that they were planning a late fitness test on Wade, but if so, they were pushing it. I started trying to prepare myself mentally for the match. I was obviously nervous. We were playing France in the opening game of the Five Nations. It was a big, big game, against a very tough side with one of the very best packs in the world. Not long after I arrived at the team's base, Geoff Cooke came over and told me what I guess I already knew. In a *Boy's Own* story I would have felt immensely proud, thrilled and exhilarated, and those feelings were in there somewhere. The main thing running through my head, though, was what the hell the line-out calls were.

On the morning of the game there was a meeting for forwards in Brian Moore's room. I made sure I was there early and while we waited for the other guys to show up, he started chatting with me about his own debut, just trying to put

'Some people just demand to be followed. Others look at them and know only that they want to be in their gang or their team. It is a safer place to be.' Michael Aylwin, *Guardian*, November 2003

me at ease. 'You're going to be terrified out there for the first five or ten minutes,' he said. 'But then you'll realise it is just another game of rugby, you'll find you are doing OK and you'll realise you can handle it.' That was an excellent confidence booster for me.

I remember getting to the old West Stand at Twickenham and climbing off the team bus alongside Will Carling, Rory Underwood and Rob Andrew, with hundreds of England fans milling around, slapping their backs as they walked by. My back went pretty much unslapped though – I was just some bloke they didn't really know. It would probably have been worse if I had been selected to play in my own right. I would have had two weeks of media pressure, of thinking about it, and I would certainly have been more nervous. In fact, apart from the complete lack of training or preparation with the team, it was not a bad way to make your debut.

France got ahead early, attacking us from the off and scoring two tries. This was quite shocking, given that England had not lost since 1990 in a championship game. There was no panic in the team, though. We just met under the posts and Will calmly talked about what we needed to do. I suffered a concussion early on, clashing heads with the prop, Laurent Seigne, in a ruck. You stayed on the pitch in those days and I remember groggily coming round, believing I was watching the match on TV. You manage to get by on autopilot, not realising you are concussed until you clear your head, but with twenty minutes to go, I finally came to.

I was jumping against Abdelatif Benazzi. He was a very athletic guy, they had been throwing quite a few short line-outs and he had won quite a bit of ball against me. His partner, Olivier Roumat, was having a good game against Martin Bayfield, too. In fact, so much so that, on our own throw, they eventually had to turn to me. Benazzi was good at jumping for his own ball, but was not so used to competing for the opposition's, so I started to win a few. We ended up taking the match by just a point, but everyone was disappointed with the way we had played.

Back at home on the Sunday, I read through the papers. A few of the journos seemed to think I had played OK and there was that sense of breakthrough. In the space of three days, I had gone from being a club player who had some potential, to playing for England.

GRAND SLAMS

1995

The 1994–95 season was a big one for England. Internationally, we had targeted a Five Nations Grand Slam to send ourselves off to the World Cup in the best possible way.

Our first game, in Dublin, was the windiest I have ever known. We could barely stand up straight during the anthems. We played into it in the first half and had no choice but to play quick and direct; there was no point kicking for territory. We won well, tearing into the Irish from the start.

Next, we faced a French side which had recently beaten New Zealand in Auckland and South Africa in Johannesburg – two tough and very rare feats. However, they had not beaten England anywhere since 1988, and we were determined to keep our run going. We mauled them all over

the pitch, but it was by no means a forward-led victory. Our backs played very well, with a try by Guscott and a brace from Tony Underwood in the final five minutes – one a move straight off the training ground that I thought would never work – giving us a 31–10 win. It was our eighth successive victory over them and the biggest since 1914.

Then to Cardiff and the old Arms Park – a stadium with great atmosphere and tremendous singing from the fans when the Welsh got on top, as they had tended to do over the years. England had won there only once since 1963, but the great days of Welsh rugby were coming to an end and we turned them over, winning 23–9.

As we were celebrating our win, we heard the news that Scotland had won in Paris, which meant they would be coming to Twickenham for the Grand Slam. There was plenty of build up to the match in the press and I felt pretty

nervous ahead of it. But it was something of an anti-climactic game which we never looked like losing. We failed to score any tries but beat them 24-12, with Rob Andrew kicking seven penalties and a drop goal. Still, a win is a win, and when it brings you a Grand Slam you don't care too much about style.

I had had something of a dream start to my England Test career, playing in just one losing match to Ireland. The World Cup beckoned.

2003

The Six Nations Grand Slam – something we felt we absolutely had to win this year.

This time we would first meet France at Twickenham. We had been beaten in Paris the year before, with their back row playing well and putting a lot of pressure on Jonny. It had finished two tries all, but we had been unable to reel them in after they got away early on. There was a lot of pressure building before the game. If we had lost to France after beating the Big Three it would have been a big, big blow and our Six Nations would have ended along with, possibly, a few careers.

We had the best of it early on, enabling Jonny to kick us ahead, but then Hodgson had a clearance kick charged down and Magne scored to bring them back into the game. At half-time it was wide open. Jason Robinson scored in the second half and we should have opened up that gap but, with nothing to lose, they came back strong and scored a pair of tries to get within eight points of us. We held on, but Will Greenwood summed the performance up when he said that the second half had been the worst England performance he had been a part of. It was a strange feeling because we had now beaten the other four of the top five teams in the world in consecutive games, albeit at home, and yet we still felt we had not really clicked. I guess that was a positive thing.

Next up we travelled to Cardiff. We had scored heavily against them in recent years, but this was never going to be that sort of game. They were almost in damage limitation mode, defending aggressively and giving away penalties if necessary to prevent try-scoring opportunities. In the end, after a dogged performance, we ran out 26-9 winners. A lot of people felt this was a disappointment for England and a moral victory for Wales. We were fairly pleased with the result, however.

By now Kay was thirty-eight weeks pregnant and the doctors had decided to induce her. The plan was to take her in on the Monday morning, the day after the Italy match. Clive gave me the week off to spend at home and it meant I didn't play in every game of the Grand Slam effort. The first twenty minutes or so of the Italy game showed England playing fantastic, mistake-free rugby but as the

game wore on the performance level dipped as Italy retained the ball and kept the score down to a respectable 40-5.

In the Scotland game, again we started well and they had two guys sin-binned. The Scots played quite well with two men down, defending with intensity and working hard for each other. Then we went down to fourteen and the game lost a little of its shape. It was fairly close until Matt Dawson tap-tackled Bryan Redpath as he went to clear and Ben Cohen leapt on the loose ball to score. After that Jason got home for a pair of tries and the game finished 40-9.

And so it was on to Dublin for England's fourth away Grand Slam decider in five years. To beat the Irish in Dublin, we would need to play with precision, pace and passion, cutting out mistakes and putting away our chances. At this point, Clive was quick to re-emphasise the importance of the Grand Slam. This was a must-win game. You couldn't have written the script of what had happened

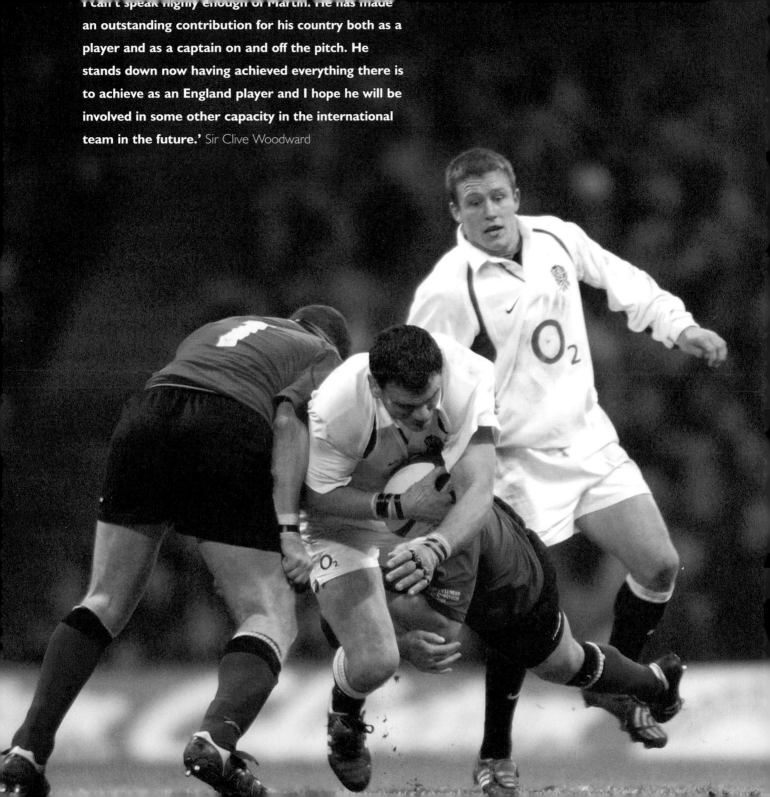

'I can't speak highly enough of Martin. He has made an outstanding contribution for his country both as a player and as a captain on and off the pitch. He stands down now having achieved everything there is to achieve as an England player and I hope he will be involved in some other capacity in the international team in the future.' Sir Clive Woodward

to the team over the previous four years. There was no way we could allow the same thing to happen in 2003. Ireland were a good side and of all the teams we had played in Grand Slam deciders, I think this was probably the best one.

I have always enjoyed playing at Lansdowne Road. It is one of the smaller stadiums – small, personal, with a vociferous and partisan crowd. I have never lost there, either. I led the guys out for the anthems. We lined up on the right-hand side as we walked out, in front of the red carpet. In the background, the crowd were giving us plenty of banter and grief, and then the Ireland team tentatively started walking behind us. Then some guy with a walkie-talkie and a tie on walked up to me. 'Johnno,' he said. 'You've gotta move the fellas. You're standing in the wrong place.' I said, 'What? We're not moving.' A bit petty, maybe, but why should we? We had run out and stood towards the end we would be defending. The crowd, who had

obviously worked out what was going on, started booing and whistling. It had become a stand-off and Backy was in my ear going, 'No, Johnno, you can't concede on this. Don't concede…don't concede.' Thanks mate. Eventually the officials gave up. The Irish lads stood to the side, their president came out to meet the teams and it was all over.

They started well, with Humphries dropping a goal after four minutes, but we responded with a try, Matt Dawson turning their ball over for Lawrence Dallaglio to score after we pressurised their scrum. We managed to repel intense Irish pressure before half time, Jonny Wilkinson putting in a massive hit on Kevin Maggs. He also dropped two right-footed goals, the second bang on the whistle. It meant we went in 13–6 ahead at half-time, with the breeze at our backs for the final forty.

The game was in the balance after the restart and had they scored it might have changed the outcome. A few mistakes crept into our play and we seemed unable to kill the game off, but once Mike Tindall touched down, the match was ours at 20-6. Will Greenwood darted over for his first try and then intercepted Geordan Murphy to score another to really silence the crowd. Danny Luger put the final nail in their coffin right at the death. The Irish boys kept going right to the end, counter-attacking and trying to score, but we held them out, winning 42-6.

In the changing room, at last, there was jubilation and a feeling of release. I looked around at the guys and was more pleased for them than for myself. We had finally laid our Grand Slam ghost and we had done it in style, playing our best game of the season.

The Big Three

In the summer of 2000 England were due to go to South Africa for a two-Test tour, complete with three midweek

'England's relentless pursuit of the elusive goal never abated for one second. From the moment Martin Johnson refused to bow to the petty protocol and change line-up positions for the national anthems, England bossed the Lansdowne turf.'
Mick Cleary, *Daily Telegraph*, March 2003

games. Six years earlier, we had won three and lost five on a similar visit. Six or seven months after Jannie de Beer had kicked us out of the 1999 World Cup, this would be a good opportunity to see how far we had progressed in relation to the Springboks.

The first Test was at Loftus Versfeld in Pretoria. The game was fairly even, with Danny Luger picking and going for a try and the South Africans keeping the board ticking over themselves. In Jonny Wilkinson's absence, Tim Stimpson had

'In a team of great players, Martin Johnson has been England's most influential over the last ten years. He played the game with an uncompromising attitude and his presence reigned supreme within the teams that he led. During the match he was an imposing figure, but afterwards always great company.

'It is a tribute to his passion and durability that he has been able to maintain such high standards over the duration of his career. At a time when his competitors were well ensconced in more comfortable retirement he was playing the best rugby of his life and leading his team to World Cup glory. The World Cup success of 2003 will always be the definitive moment in an outstanding career.

'Congratulations Martin on a wonderful career; it has been a pleasure to walk part of the journey on the opposite side.' John Eales, former Australian captain and RWC winner

'I remember that last game – the World Cup final. We were in the tunnel about to enter the cauldron of Telstra Stadium. The teams were lined up and I wondered what Johnno would say to us. Previously in this situation before a game, Johnno had always turned around and offered one final call to arms. He has the capacity to shock us and intimidate opponents with his venom and aggression and I wondered if once again this is what we would see. But Johnno was far smarter than that. He turned around, fixed us with that beetle-browed stare and began to open his mouth. But for the first time he said nothing. That silence counted for a thousand words. He could see in our eyes that we were ready. I still wonder what that must have felt like for Australia.' Jonny Wilkinson

'Martin was an outstanding competitor at international level. On the field he played the game hard and he's a good bloke off it. Over the years, be it with England, the Lions, and then ultimately in the Rugby World Cup final, it was always competitive but good-natured between us.

'As player and captain he commanded respect from his team-mates and opposition alike. He is a true leader and I wish him all the best for his testimonial season.' George Gregan, captain of the Wallabies

come on to the wing to kick goals. We had got ourselves into a good field position and the ball was kicked through for Stimmo to chase. He raced ahead of

Andre Vos and as the ball bounced high over the line he looked to have got his hand on it and appeared to have just got it down, with Vos tackling him in the process. My view at the time was that it was a try – I think that to this day – but it went to the video referee. I looked across at the referee and said, 'We're not going to get given this. Let's just carry on with the game.' The decision came back a few moments later: knock-on, scrum to South Africa. A tough one to take, but there's nothing you can do.

With ten minutes to go, I had to come off as I was feeling sick and dehydrated and had stomach cramps. Lawrence played in the second row for the final few minutes and I watched as the Boks potted a penalty to win it 18–13. It was pretty disappointing. I'm sure that, if the Stimpson try had been allowed, we would have gone on to win the game.

We flew up to Bloemfontein for the second Test and by the time the game came around we were feeling refreshed and ready and looking forward to the challenge. The first twenty minutes were really quick. The game was whizzing along, everyone just reacting to what was going on. As it developed, though, we started to exert some control, with Jonny kicking his penalties and dropping a goal while a sin-binning had us down to fourteen men. Right at the death there was another controversial video referee moment: we were leading 27-15 but they put pressure on us and a ruck developed right on our line. With people lying everywhere, van der Westhuizen stuck his hand into the dark mass of bodies and claimed a try. You couldn't see the ball and in my opinion there was no way it could be given. But it was. They converted and were back in the match at 27-22 but we just knew we were going to win. As injury time ticked away I was knocked out of the line-out. The referee awarded us a penalty and there was that lovely feeling that all we needed to do was put the ball dead and the game was ours. Five metres from

the touchline, Jonny swings his left boot and it is all over.

It was the start of our great run against South Africa and, indeed, the rest of the southern-hemisphere sides, right through the Rugby World Cup 2003, we didn't lose to any of them, home or away.

Our next southern hemisphere matches were going to be that autumn, with games against Australia and, once again, South Africa, at Twickenham. The first game, against the Wallabies, was the big one. They were world champions, they rarely came to the UK and everyone wanted to see how we would go against them.

We took some time to settle, perhaps shading the set piece and winning, statistically, the battles for possession and territory. But, as we had tended to do against the Big Three over the years, we were failing to make the best use of it. They changed their tactics in the second half, playing directly, with a lot of pick-

'One thing about me is that I will always be known as an honest person. Not only is Johnno the best captain I have played under at international level, but he also happens to be the best-looking skipper of all time. He could grace any catwalk around the world and he would not be out of place on the front cover of *Vogue*. Okay, I guess one of the two points I mentioned is not true ...

'MJ is an exceptional player and a captain. He leads by example – he might not say much, but when he talks you listen; as he never talks for the sake of talking. Everyone respected him at all times, mainly because he would never ask you to do something that he would not do himself. While he is not a man of words – he would let his action do the talking.

'He always had the potential from a young age to become a very good player, his will to win was always evident. That will to win is still evident in Johnno, even though he has retired from international rugby and it's a testament to him that he is still playing the kind of rugby that he is today.

'Johnno – all the best for your testimonial year. Nobody deserves it more and I hope it goes brilliantly for you.' Jason Leonard, former England and Lions team-mate and fellow RWC winner and-go from the forwards, and rapidly scored. You could feel the crowd drop a notch but the players didn't let their heads go down and the turning point came when Clive threw on Iain Balshaw. At this point, you could see the Wallabies were tired. In contrast, Balshaw, very much on the up, was fresh, bubbling with confidence and raring to go. If we could get the ball to him, I knew he could do some damage with his pace. The crucial moment came deep in injury time. With the Wallabies in front, he saw some space and chipped ahead. If the ball went dead, I was sure the whistle would sound. Then Dan Luger raced through the Aussie defenders and touched down. It went to the video referee. The score would be 20-19 to us if the call went our way. The roar from the crowd told me which way the ref had gone. Jonny didn't miss and the game was over.

Next up was Argentina, which turned out to be a pretty poor game which we won 19-0. Then it was on to South

Africa. The Boks were more familiar to us than the Wallabies, though they were trying to move away from their traditional, pack-dominated game to a more free-flowing style. It was a physical game and it was played at a hell of a pace. They defended well, but after half an hour or so Will Greenwood broke through the line and stepped round the full-back to score. We won 25-17, but there were no over-the-top celebrations in the changing room, which was good. It reflected the fact that we were starting to believe in ourselves. Before, beating South Africa would have been a huge thing. Now we knew we could do it and that it wasn't a one-off.

The autumn of 2001 once again brought the Australians and South Africans to Twickenham. For the Wallabies game a number of senior players were missing, myself included, with a broken hand failing to mend in time. The boys had a great first half, the forwards pushing the Australians back and forcing them to give away penalties

that Jonny duly converted into points. England went in 15-0 up at the break but the Wallabies came back strongly and when Phil Waugh touched down to make it 21-15 to England, they looked like they might force their way back into contention. However, the guys hung on well to win and retain the Cook Cup.

I was back for the visit of South Africa and this turned into a surprisingly comfortable victory – and allowed us to become the first European nation to record five successive wins against southern hemisphere teams. The Boks made a lot of mistakes and Jonny made them pay. We won 29-9 and as I'd only played one club game since breaking my hand, it was nice to come back and get through a physical Test match.

With the World Cup looming large on the horizon, the autumn 2002 internationals took on extra significance – especially as we were playing host to the Big Three on consecutive weekends. First up were New Zealand but the

match started poorly for us, with Jonah touching down in the corner after he got on the end of a movement which stretched right across the field. I was disappointed that they scored; they were close to our line and with little space to work in I felt we should have been able to cut them off. They had carried out a move where the ball had been passed behind a player's back and we had been caught out. In the English Premiership, this was something that was always penalised and therefore not something we had worked on defending. However, the South African referee let it go and it raised the old questions about consistency between north and south. Amazingly, by the time we returned to our clubs, the tactic was commonplace. I welcomed this turn-about, because I think it gives attackers more opportunity to break defensive lines.

We managed to apply some pressure and Jonny kicked penalties to keep us in the game, but after we managed to turn over their ball and counter-attack they

intercepted a pass, got the ball out to Doug Howlett and he managed to out-run Jason Robinson to the line. Now we were two tries down. This was not a position we found ourselves in often and it was highly annoying, especially given that we pride ourselves on our defence. We managed to pull a try back but it was not a happy changing room at half-time. I thought we looked rusty and hesitant. I wanted us to run powerfully at them. 'If in doubt, let's go forward aggressively and commit defenders,' I said. My thinking was that if we took them on, the chances to power through tackles or offload in the tackle would come. And after the restart, things improved. Wilko chipped over the defence and re-gathered to score, Ben Cohen smashed through to the line. 31-14, with the conversion. We ought to have accelerated from there, but the game was far from over. They came back at us, Lomu scoring the type of try only he can and their replacement scrum-half also scored. 31-28 with ten minutes to go. At the death, they got down to our corner and thank God Benny Kay managed to steal their line-out ball on our line and that kept the game safe for us. We had beaten the All Blacks for the first time in nine years.

We scarcely had time to recover our breath before the Wallabies arrived. It was a similar game in many ways. We started OK, with Jonny kicking a few goals, and we grabbed the first try. They got back into it, but at 16-6 up in first-half injury time we looked good. Then Jonny slipped on our line and Elton Flatley nipped through to touch down, meaning we turned round 16-13 up. The previous week, the beginning of the second half had been our time but now it was reversed as the Australians had a dream start. Instead of being comfortable, we found ourselves comfortably behind 28-16. As Flatley scored his second conversion we gathered under the posts and recognised that we had started to be a little too restrained, too conscious of getting into trouble with the referee.

'Martin Johnson; I've known him since he was seventeen years old. I've played in various teams with him and he is the greatest leader I have ever played under. In fact, I think he is probably the greatest rugby player the world has ever seen – without trying to suck up to him too much! There were a lot of heroes from the World Cup, but he is one of the few who really deserves his accolades. If he had not been England's captain I don't think they would have won the World Cup – as simple as that.

'His strength is that he leads by example. I've played under a lot of captains in my time; he doesn't say much, but his actions speak volumes for him. If you get a captain who's always talking and nagging at you he becomes like a little dog yapping in the corner and you just ignore him. Johnno is like a big dog that barks loudly every now and then and you take note.

'I'm delighted that he's been awarded a testimonial season as he's one of the true greats of the game and I wish him all the best.'
Graham Rowntree, Leicester team-mate and former England and Lions colleague

Down a lot of points, with nothing to lose, we agreed to be more direct, more assertive in our approach, and it started to pay dividends. We made progress up the field, continuing to kick our goals and although we were behind on the scoreboard we were starting to get on top. We were the fitter team, you could see them looking at the clock, blowing hard, hands on knees. That boosted us and when Sinbad dummied to send Ben Cohen in under the posts on a beautifully timed and angled run, Jonny converted and suddenly we were 32-31 ahead. The crowd, exhilarated by our comeback, were starting to make a lot of noise. We were now defending our slender lead, playing for territory, keeping them out of drop goal or penalty range. Injury time seemed to stretch on for ever but fortunately our defence was strong and we kept them out to win.

And so, a week later, it was on to the final Test: South Africa. The week before, South Africa had been beaten 21–6 by Scotland, their first loss to the Scots since

1969. That meant two things: firstly, that the pressure was on us to win and to win well and, secondly, that the Springboks were likely to come out fighting.

Our suspicion that they would be emotional about the Scotland defeat was proved correct because, as they ran out at Twickenham, several of them hung around on the halfway line, squaring up to us and shouting things in Afrikaans as we made our way on to the field. The lock, Jannes Labuschagne, was one of them and he singled me out for a few stares and threats. Obviously, I couldn't understand what he was saying, but perhaps it was, 'I'm gonna get sent off after twenty minutes! Got that, you muppet?'

I remember thinking that this was going to be interesting and it was nasty from the start. The first time Jason Robinson got the ball he was punched, Jonny came in for a bit of treatment and one or two other fists went flying in. The thing that really irritated me was when the referee called me and Krigé together. 'Listen, guys,' he said. 'Both teams have got to calm down. The next guy to cross the line is off.' I said, 'Mate, we haven't done anything.' Within minutes, though, Labuschagne had blatantly followed through on Wilkinson. It was not the worst incident of the day – if he had done it in the first minute of a game he might not even have been carded – but in the circumstances, the referee was absolutely right to send him off.

The consensus of opinion, post-match, seemed to be that the red card ruined the game; with fourteen men on the field the Boks had no chance of winning. My response is that Leicester went on to lose to Bristol at the end of the 2002-03 season when Bristol were down to fourteen men for seventy-five minutes, so it can be done.

We tried as best we could to keep some structure on the play – they had some dangerous runners – and I felt that the more the game broke down and

became an unstructured mess the more chance they had to come back at us. We didn't want that, we wanted to turn the screw, and as the game wore on we managed to do it. It ended 53–3, with us pushing them over their own line from a five-metre scrum. I knew they wouldn't like that.

So, as they jetted off and we sat down to count our bruises, we could at least reflect on a successful autumn. We had beaten all of the Big Three, one after the other, and no team had ever done that before. Against the Springboks, the match will always be remembered for the thuggery rather than the rugby, but the record books show we put fifty points on them and that proves how far English rugby had come in ten years.

The World Cup would obviously be the main event in 2003, but as part one of the biggest and final hurdle of our long international season, we would be playing back-to-back Tests away in New Zealand and Australia. For the game in

Wellington, at the so-called 'Cake Tin' Stadium, we picked the same team as we had for the Grand Slam decider against Ireland.

We started poorly, allowing them to make breaks and being pinged for offences at the ruck – we were probably lucky to avoid having players binned in the first half. As ever, Jonny kept us in touch and we went in at 6-6. The second half started better. I felt we were getting into the game more and starting to play. Disaster loomed, however, when first Neil Back and then Lawrence Dallaglio were yellow-carded. We were down to thirteen men and the All Blacks had a penalty close to our posts. They made the sensible decision to go for the scrum and push us over: simple maths really, eight against six. With the crowd screaming, at first in delight and then in disbelief, we kept them out with a fantastic effort from the front row. Graham Rowntree, particularly, had worked incredibly hard to keep them from manoeuvring the scrum into such a

position that their No. 8 could pick and go. Graham was penalised for his efforts, they took a quick tap and we prevented them scoring again. Their moment was gone.

With the ball in our hands, we concentrated on doing the simple things well. We started going forward, playing good rugby and actually claimed three points of our own through a Jonny drop-goal. Suddenly we were back up to fifteen men again and although Howlett scored later from a kick ahead, we were in front and we stayed there. It finished 15-13 and for the first time in thirty years, we had beaten the All Blacks in New Zealand.

It took two or three days to get over the Wellington match and feel like playing a Test again. England had never beaten the Wallabies in Australia, which gave the build up a little extra spice. We were pretty whacked after a very long season, but we refused to admit it. The game was played indoors at the Telstra

Dome and whether the roof was responsible or not, it was certainly a quick game, exploding from the kick-off, with the ball pinging everywhere. The Aussies were breaking from their own third, but we were first to draw blood, through Will Greenwood and then, with great hands, through Mike Tindall.

We had a good lead at half-time and the danger was in thinking, 'What do we do next?' The answer was, 'Keep playing the same way,' but for the first twenty minutes of the second half we were lethargic and errors crept into our game, allowing them a foothold. I was starting to worry a bit, and then – bang! – Ben Cohen blasted through the middle to score and take us out of reach. They managed to pull one back through Wendell Sailor, which was disappointing as we would have loved to have nilled them for tries. However, a 25-14 scoreline looked pretty good.

And so, on 21 June 2003, our international season was finally over.

Ten matches played, ten won, including two massive games won away from 'Fortress Twickenham'. The question on everyone's lips was: 'What does it all mean for the World Cup?' We know now.

WORLD CUPS

1995

The 1995 Rugby World Cup was a massive turning point in rugby. It was the third World Cup and it took off in a really big way, increasing the sport's global profile hugely as a result. South Africa was a great place to hold the tournament – an exciting, exotic, rugby-mad country with impressive stadiums packed with fans from around the world.

We had flown in with reasonable hopes. England had been beaten finalists in 1991 and a number of players were left from that team, with some good young guys in there too. However, it didn't

'Sat in front of my telly this summer watching the proceedings of our England team on their demanding tour of the southern hemisphere was when I finally began to realise how good Martin Osborne Johnson actually was. Halfway through the second Test I picked up my phone and wrote the following text – "You are a bloody legend!" – looked up in my address book, not you Austin, the name Johnno and sent it off hoping this would go some way to showing how highly I regard Martin as both a colleague and a friend. You see, it took me back twelve months to when I believe we actually won the World Cup. Wellington, New Zealand was the venue. Sure, we had won the Grand Slam and beaten the big boys on our own patch – but we had never convinced anyone on foreign soil. Two men in the sin bin, Rockocoko, Spencer, Howlett and friends ready to put us to the sword, when Captain Marvel dragged us up by our lapels and convinced us we could win, not in word but in deed. It was an honour to be on the same field as him that day, immense does not do him justice. How we could have done with him this summer. Yet afterwards he spoke of teamwork, organisation and structure, the team man to the fore once more. Then, when asked what was going through his mind when the All Blacks had their fourth consecutive scrum on our try line with only six men in the pack, he replied with a deadpan face – "My arse!" In that one day he encapsulated everything that is Martin Johnson; a quite simply magnificent player, a leader to be proud of, and a man with tremendous wit.

'Just in case Johnno didn't get my text, "Johnno – you are a bloody legend!"'

England and Lions team-mate Will Greenwood

start very well. In fact we could have lost
to Argentina in our opener and weren't
that impressive against Italy. We only
really seemed to get going when we
picked a young side with some good
second-string guys to play Samoa in our
last pool game, which we won.

Our spirits were high. Our weakest team
had secured our best win and we were
off to the quarter-final as pool winners,
where we would face the world
champion Wallabies. It was a fast-paced
game from the start. We edged ahead
through a sixty-yard Tony Underwood
try and at half time Jack Rowell came on
to the pitch to speak to us. 'Don't you
lose this game now, don't you lose this
bloody game,' he kept saying. This was
sound advice from the big man, but
straight after the restart they scored. The
game went backwards and forwards
from there until it was tied right at the
death. As extra time beckoned we had a
line-out on the left-hand side of the field.
Martin Bayfield got the ball, we made
some yards and Dewi Morris got it out

to Rob, who smashed over a monster
drop-goal and ran round the pitch with a
silly grin on his face. And we were
through to the semi-finals.

You could feel the hype from the press,
who were getting ahead of themselves
and talking about finals, but I am
something of a pessimist and I had my
doubts about whether we could
triumph over the All Blacks. They had
beaten Scotland the week before pretty
comfortably, with a guy called Jonah
Lomu doing a fair bit of damage.

The game kicked off and everything was
fairly normal for about sixty seconds.
Then the ball was pinged out to Lomu
on the left wing and he bust through
three or four tackles to score. From the
kick-off, Walter Little smashed through
Jerry Guscott and Josh Kronfeld
touched down, after a move which
travelled almost the length of the field,
for their second try. Lomu broke
through the middle to touch down
again minutes later and inside the first

quarter the game was already virtually lost. I have never felt so powerless, so impotent, on a rugby field. We managed to come back into it a bit, with both Will and Rory scoring a pair of tries, but the final score, 45–29, flattered us. I guess they had relaxed with the result in the bag. Our World Cup dream was over that year.

1999

The build-up to the 1999 World Cup tournament was like nothing I have experienced before or since. Back in England after an exhausting summer training camp on South Stradbrooke Island, a fifteen-minute boat ride off Queensland's Gold Coast, we continued with our training, spending the whole of the summer and early autumn together, working hard on our fitness and skills. We were probably stronger and fitter than we have ever been, but we felt a massive weight of expectation on all of our shoulders.

We weren't favourites for the tournament. We weren't even near-favourites. A semi-final spot would have been a fair result, but because we had beaten the Boks in the autumn, the press were building us up, and instead of enjoying what we were doing and giving it our best shot, we slowly got sucked in. We beat Italy 67–7 in our opening game and then turned our attention to the All Blacks. We probably had the better of the possession and territory in the first ten or fifteen minutes, but they scored first, Jonah Lomu bashing through our defence, allowing Tana Umaga to run to the line and offload to Jeff Wilson to get over in the corner. Phil de Glanville got one back for us in the second half, pouncing on a loose ball that bounced back from the posts after a kick ahead. We were maybe in the ascendant at that point, but the key moment was another Lomu score, the kind of try only he can produce, with tacklers flying everywhere on his run in. That took the wind out of our sails and as we tried to force the pace to come

back, Byron Kelleher got over again to make it 30–16. We had battled hard – you couldn't question the guys' effort or commitment – but it wasn't enough.

Our World Cup chances died that day. Although we beat Tonga comfortably by 101–10 in our final pool game, we now faced a play-off match against Fiji just five days afterwards, with the quarter-final, against South Africa, only four days further on. It was an impossible schedule. We defeated the Fijians 45–24, but were picking up injuries along the way and had no time to rehab them properly and no time for general rest.

On the Thursday, we had to travel to Paris and that left two days to recover and prepare for the Springboks. In contrast, their pool had been fairly simple. Their squad players had all had a good run out and they were mentally and physically fresh, whereas guys like myself and Lawrence had started every game and we were all knackered. I think that showed in the match.

The first half was fairly cagey, with both sides kicking a lot of ball, but once they nosed ahead we had nothing left, although we fought as hard as we could, we just weren't able to come back at them. Jannie de Beer applied the killer blows to our World Cup with a world record five, sweetly struck drop goals soaring over our heads. The final score, 44–21, was pretty shattering and fairly emphatic. There were no two ways about it: we were out of the World Cup and on the way home the next morning.

2003

It's every rugby player's dream to lift the World Cup, but no England side had come close to doing so since 1991.

With that single final appearance, then, our Rugby World Cup record had, some felt, been one of under-achievement. Many critics felt that was about to change. The Zurich Rankings, based on results in the previous twelve months,

said we were the world's number one team – and had us going into the tournament as favourites. We had had a good summer. We had worked very hard and we got on the plane to Australia feeling fit, confident and looking forward to the start of the tournament.

There had been a lot of talk before the tournament started about how, as one of the older teams, we might feel the heat but that didn't worry me unduly: most of our matches would be played in the relative cool of the evening to coincide with TV scheduling in Europe.

We were lucky that Georgia were our first opponents, rather than South Africa or Samoa. Lacking a little match fitness and sharpness, we needed to get a game under our belts. Although we won by 84-6, it was by no means easy: they were big, physical guys and they flew into the tackles with relish.

It was a strange week – Clive later said it was the most stressful and anxious seven days he had known in rugby to that point and I have to agree. There was no getting away from the events of a year before, our 53-3 defeat of South Africa at Twickenham amid a flurry of flying elbows, knees and fists. Our World Cup encounter had been looming since that match.

Unusually in the history of encounters between England and South Africa, we went into the match as very strong favourites to win it. That just added to the enormous pressure and nervousness that the whole team was feeling. If we had lost it would have been a huge downer: we had flown out as the world's best team, on paper, and in a pretty confident mood. If we lost, it would have made our progress in the World Cup much harder.

It was a tough game, as we had known it would be. We started brightly, making forays down their wings, but they applied pressure and we started to give away penalties. Fortunately their fly-half, Louis Koen, missed three kicks at goals in the first half and the score was level 6-6 as we went in at half-time.

The turning point came when Lewis Moody charged down a clearance kick by Koen and Will Greenwood raced on to the rebound to score. Jonny converted and then dropped a goal fairly quickly afterwards. At that point you could feel the wind go out of their sails as they realised they were not going to win. They rallied though, and nearly scored at the end, but by the time the final whistle went we had racked up nineteen unanswered points to take the result 25-6.

The Australian press were, predictably, unimpressed. 'Is That All You've Got?' ran one headline, over a picture of Jonny kicking another penalty. In many ways, it was a compliment: this was the Springboks we'd beaten, after all, and nineteen points was not a small margin.

From the sunshine of Perth, we headed for the rain and cloud of Melbourne. All of the pressure of the South Africa week had evaporated to be replaced by a flat feeling as we looked ahead to Samoa. They would be straining at the leash – an unnerving thought when you look at the size and physicality of some of their guys – and this would almost be their 'final'. But whatever we said to ourselves, we struggled to believe it; with the toughest game of the pool stages out of the way, it was almost as though the job had been done and all we had to do now was get the next two matches over and done with.

We were rudely awakened within the first few minutes of the kick-off. Samoa played fantastic rugby, spinning the ball very wide and running it at us from deep inside their twenty-two. They scored one of the best tries of the tournament, a flowing move in which virtually every player seemed to touch the ball about five times. We were 10-0 down and it felt like we were chasing shadows. At that point I was seriously worried: if they were going to carry on playing mistake-free rugby at that pace, we were going to struggle. On sixty minutes they still had the lead, at 22-20, though by this point I did at least feel we would win – I was sure we could get into their half and score enough points to take us clear. When Iain Balshaw scored from a lovely Wilkinson cross kick and Phil Vickery dummied over from close range for his first international try, we knew the game was safe.

No doubt about it, though, Samoa gave us a real fright. They had had everything to gain and nothing to lose: if they tried something and it came off, great. If it didn't, and we scored a try, so what? People expected that. Freed from those shackles, they played the game of their tournament, a game the World Cup needed.

Luckily, our next match was against Uruguay. The dice were always heavily loaded against the South Americans.

They were a team of amateurs and those sides will always struggle to live with any of the world's top teams; they can hold their own in the tight, particularly early on, but they can't compete once the ball goes wide and the fast backs start to open them up. Despite their frankly impossible playing schedule prior to meeting us, they were very game and they worked hard, but there was no way they would come close to competing in those circumstances and we ran out 111-13 winners.

We came off the field nursing our bumps and bruises and mentally starting to prepare to face the Welsh the following week. Although we felt that our attack would get through their defence, we knew they had a good attacking game which was capable of causing us problems too. But we didn't expect the problems to be as serious as they were. They absorbed our early pressure and hit us on the counter-attack to run up a ten-point lead in the

first half. We made plenty of breaks of our own, but somehow weren't managing to turn them into tries.

Half-time felt awful: welcome to my nightmare. There were not many smiles in the dressing room. All around I could see a lot of very tired guys. I was struggling myself. If we had been fresh, I would not have worried. We would be able to outlast them. As it was, I honestly wondered whether we had the energy to come back. The unthinkable seemed horribly possible: an exit in the quarter-final.

But a good piece of tactical thinking by Woody helped to rescue the situation. Clive brought Mike Tindall off for Mike Catt, gambling that Catty's fresh legs, kicking skills and ability to step in as first receiver would help take pressure off Wilko. When Jason Robinson made a dazzling run through almost the entire Welsh defence to put Will Greenwood in for a converted try we were back to 10-10 in quick time. From that point I

didn't think we would lose, and we scored twenty-five points to seven – with Jonny knocking over a number of penalties – to win that second half comprehensively and the match reasonably comfortably. It had been anything but the cakewalk some pundits had been expecting, though. We were privately critical of ourselves, thinking that we should have scored more than once and we shouldn't have conceded.

With New Zealand beating South Africa, Australia defeating the Scots, and France coming out on top against Ireland, the four semi-finalists were known, with us facing France. Up until the semi-final we had been expected to beat teams heavily and to do it in style. Now we had reverted to type, the experts were saying, relying on keeping the ball tight and using Jonny's boot to grind out the wins. The French, meanwhile, had snuck up on the rails almost unseen. Suddenly everyone was sitting up and raving about them and the effect was that they became the favourites for our semi-final.

We were extremely concerned about how tired we had been at the break in the Wales game, and as a result we had a rethink about our training schedule. This helped us keep a sharpness and freshness to what we were doing and the week went really well.

As we drove to Sydney's Telstra Stadium for our semi-final with France, the skies got greyer and greyer and the threatened rain arrived. The scene inside was absolutely incredible: a sea of white jerseys, England flags and banners. The place holds 80,000 people and the majority of them must have been English. It was better than Twickenham: when people are away at a sporting event, particularly in a place like Australia, they become more nationalistic, they wear their England shirts and they sing their hearts out.

By kick-off it was pouring down, very unusual in Sydney in mid-November. The French started well, winning a line-out not far from our line. We disrupted

'For the rest of that first half, England, playing the game of width that critics said they would never do in the wet, achieved a growing ascendancy. Johnson, in his finest hour, led the way with controlled fury.' David Hands, *The Times*, November 2003

their throw, but Serge Betsen did well to get his hands on the ball and did well to reach the try-line. The video ref was called in and the try was given, which Michalak converted. We didn't panic though, and got on with trying to play our game. They were defending well with plenty of bodies in the centre of the field. We tried at first to go outside those bodies but they turned us over on several occasions and it became something of a duel for territory. We turned round 12-7 ahead and produced a very strong second-half performance. It wasn't particularly pretty: we kicked a lot and put them under pressure, waiting for them to knock on or concede penalties. Then Jonny would step up and make them pay. We could see them losing heart with every three points he added. We knew we'd won it when Olivier Magne tried to kick out of his twenty-two and was sandwiched between myself and Lawrence. As he lay there on the deck he started gesturing at Lol and moaning at the ref rather than getting up. They didn't score another point after Michalak's tenth-minute conversion and it finished 24-7.

'He stood with his hands on his hips, the most perfect look of disdain on his face, as the teams stood in formation waiting the start of the second and final period of extra time.'
Michael Aylwin, *Guardian*, November 2003

We weren't jubilant – I later heard that the Wallabies went on a lap of honour after their win over the All Blacks, but we've got something of a history with laps of honour so we just headed for the changing room. Clive reflected this in his positive post-match press conference, telling the reporters that we hadn't come all this way to finish second, that we had won nothing yet and that we expected to win the dream final: Australia against England.

My main concern ahead of the final was that it should not be too hot or humid and my wish was granted: the cool and showery pattern continued. In those few moments before we came out, I just asked the players to look round at each other, at the guys with whom they had been through so many experiences. I found it very difficult to say anything profound but it wasn't necessary. It was a World Cup final, for God's sake. As we came out for the anthems, I guessed the crowd was split 60-40 in favour of Australia, an amazing effort from our fans, who were never outsung.

Australia started the game very well. We made a couple of mistakes and one of the front row was penalised for an alleged punch. They scored early when they kicked to the corner and Lote Tuqiri got up above the smaller Jason Robinson to touch down. That wasn't great, though they missed the conversion. We got back on attack quickly, going through plenty of phases but not making much inroad as their defence held firm. However, I started to feel their forwards were getting worn down: our attack was making progress and gaining momentum, and they started to give away penalties. The highlight of the half was a stunning try by Jason Robinson. Lawrence Dallaglio made it with a bursting run round a ruck, off-loading beautifully to Jonny who passed on to Jason. With a pair of Wallabies homing in on him, Robbo dived in, sliding across the line before his momentum carried him back upright,

yelling 'Come on!' and punching the ball in the air. Cue huge singing from the many thousands of England fans inside the ground.

We knew coming in how dangerous the Australian attack could be but we were keeping Sailor, Mortlock and Tuqiri pretty much in check and making a few little half-breaks ourselves. We had to watch our defence, though. As forwards, we had to concentrate hard on keeping our defensive line spot on, because there was always the risk of letting them in if a ten-metre gap appeared between me and, say, Phil Vickery.

We were making a number of silly handling errors, though, and I wasn't happy with that. One of the biggest sins in rugby is to lose possession cheaply. I seem to have spent my whole career saying 'Look after the ball, hold on to the ball, cherish the ball, worship the ball, protect the ball, look after the f**cking ball!' Here, in the World Cup final of all places, the ball seemed continually to be

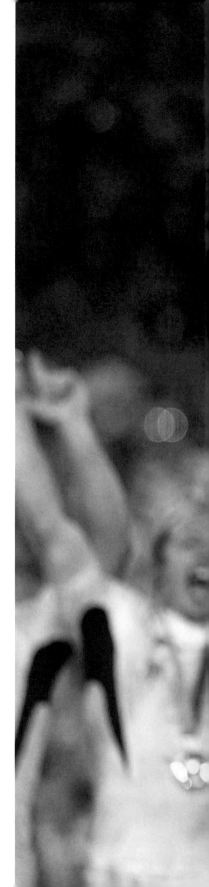

dropped or knocked on. Nevertheless, we went 5-14 up at half-time, but 5-19 or 5-21 would have felt even better and would probably have signalled the end of the game as a contest.

In a calm dressing room, we talked though a few technical points: line-outs, scrummage and how to adjust our game plan for the slight breeze we'd now face. As I sucked down some fluids, I assessed how I felt: calm, strong and full of running. The rest of the boys looked in a similar way.

We started the second half very well, nicking line-outs – though we lost a few of our own, too – and smashing them back when we tried to go forward directly. We were the stronger, more physical side but every time we got pressure on them it was the same old story – a dropped ball, a needless penalty, allowing them to claw back six precious points. Jonny tried a couple of snap drop goals but they slid wide to raucous Australian booing and we stayed

scoreless in the half as the minutes ticked away.

Suddenly, though, we found ourselves in the dying seconds of the game, still ahead 14-11. The Aussies had the put-in to a scrum, we got the shove on them and their tight-head, unable to cope, folded in. There is no doubt that referee Andre Watson should have awarded a penalty to us. Game over. Instead, he ordered the scrum be reset and then he penalised us. Right at the end of the match, Elton Flatley – nerveless under immense pressure – kicked the goal to level the scores and the final whistle went: extra time. If we had dwelt on the fact that they had potted three penalties in the second half to no points from us, despite our many opportunities, I think we might have had problems: had we just thrown away the World Cup? As it was, no one was dwelling on anything.

You think ten minutes each way is a long time but it flashes by. I'm dragged down in a line-out, Jonny slots the penalty from really long range – it was never in doubt, which lifted us and must have been like a knife in the ribs to them – and before you know it the half-time whistle sounds: 14-17. One hand back on the trophy.

The second ten starts after a minute's breather and the play moves back and forth.

'Had Johnson panicked and charged early before Back had the ball secure in his hands, the rugged Australian defence might have smashed the attack backwards and out of shape. Watch the moment again. Johnson pauses, three or four seconds, assessing, preparing himself. In the heat of the moment, he remained as cool as a hired gun.'

Stuart Barnes, *Daily Telegraph*

Ninety seconds to go: we are penalised for a nonsense rucking offence inside kicking range. Flatley, massively cool again, puts it through the posts. The score is 17-17 and we are heading for sudden death: first team to score points wins the World Cup.

Sixty seconds to go: we decide to kick long at the re-start, try to pressure them into kicking into touch and concentrate on winning the ball. A ruck forms, the Wallabies all over it like a rash. They're all watching Jonny, expecting the drop-goal. Daws spots this and realises no one's on him. Bravely he manages a sharp show-and-go to burst through. He makes ten or fifteen metres or more straight up the field.

Eventually, the scrambling Australian defence nails Daws, leaving him pinned at the bottom of the ruck. Backy gets into Daws' position and looks as though he's thinking of shipping the ball out to Wilko. I have a flash of horror – Backy spinning the ball out on the bounce or way over Wilkinson's head. I make a run, trying to catch Neil's eye and, thank God, he spots me and pops the ball up. I go nowhere and am taken to ground but it's not the distance that counts. Matt Dawson is now up and in position.

Thirty seconds to go: the ball gets squeezed back. George Gregan, acutely aware, now, that we've manufactured a perfect chance for Jonny, is yelling 'Field goal! Field goal!' Daws crouches over the ball and looks up for his fly-half.

Then it's out and Jonny swings back his wrong right foot. It's an ugly kick, they later tell me, but it's the best thing I've ever seen on a rugby field ... a tumbling, swerving punt smashed between the posts. We are in the lead again.

Running back, I glance at the clock on one of the big screens. Time is almost up so I know this is the last play of the game.

Twenty seconds to go: the Australians race back to re-start before we can get

'No plaudit too high for England's colossus. Led by example, held lineout together including one great steal from Justin Harrison. Constantly took the battle to Australia. A tower of strength with an aura of invincibility.'
Mark Souster, *The Times*, November 2003

properly into position. They kick short. They need to recover the ball because if they don't, as long as we don't infringe and give them a penalty, the Webb Ellis Trophy is on its way to Twickenham. Someone – I don't see who – catches the re-start and sets up the ruck. The ball comes back, Matt lets a few seconds tick away and then gets it out to Mike Catt, over the head of the crouching Will Greenwood who has knelt down to avoid getting in the way. Catty hoofs the ball into touch, and it's all over. Unbelievable.